# GAME DAY

# Score!

## You Can Play Soccer

by Nick Fauchald

illustrated by Bill Dickson

Thanks to our advisers for their expertise, research, and advice:

Wendy Frappier, Ph.D.
Assistant Professor, Health and Physical Education Department
Minnesota State University
Moorhead, Minnesota

Susan Kesselring, M.A., Literacy Educator
Rosemount-Apple Valley-Eagan (Minnesota) School District

PICTURE WINDOW BOOKS
Minneapolis, Minnesota

Managing Editor: Bob Temple
Creative Director: Terri Foley
Editor: Brenda Haugen
Editorial Adviser: Andrea Cascardi
Copy Editor: Laurie Kahn
Designer: Nathan Gassman
Page production: Picture Window Books
The illustrations in this book are watercolor.

Picture Window Books
5115 Excelsior Boulevard
Suite 232
Minneapolis, MN  55416
1-877-845-8392
www.picturewindowbooks.com

Printed in the United States of America.

**Library of Congress Cataloging-in-Publication Data**
Fauchald, Nick.
Score! You can play soccer / written by Nick
Fauchald ; illustrated by Bill Dickson.
p. cm. — (Game day)
Summary: A brief introduction to the game
of soccer as intended to be played by children.
Includes bibliographical references (p.    ) and index.
ISBN 1-4048-0262-2 (lib. bdg.)
1.  Soccer Juvenile literature. [1. Soccer.]
I. Dickson, Bill, 1949- ill. II. Title.
GV943.25 .F39 2004
796.334—dc22
                          2003019999

n your uniform: shorts
ny new soccer jersey.
u put on your shin
 which protect the
halves of your legs.

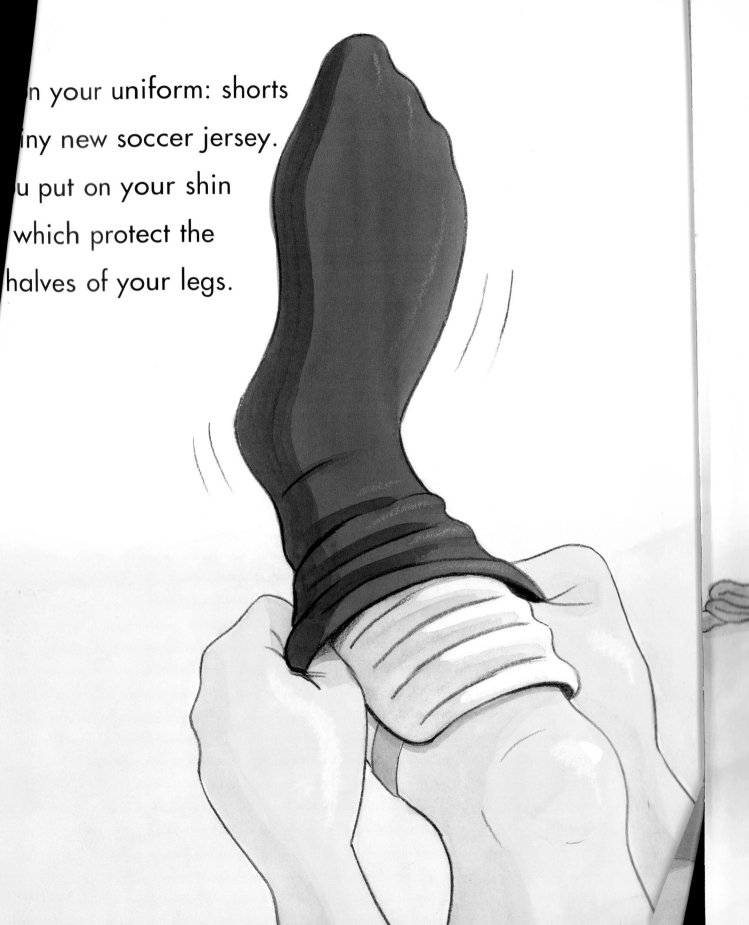

Soccer is the most popular sport in the world. Because soccer doesn't require much gear, boys and girls anywhere can enjoy it. The object of the game is to kick the soccer ball into the other team's goal and to keep the other team from kicking the ball into your goal.

Mom is smiling when she wakes you up. "It's a beautiful, sunny Saturday," she says.

"It's perfect weather for a so[c...] Time to get dressed. We have [...] soccer field in an hour."

You put [...] and a sh[...] Next, y[...] guards, [...] bottom[...]

Finally, you put on long socks over your shin guards and lace up your cleats. Cleats are special shoes that have bumps on the bottom so you won't slip on the grass.

In most countries, soccer is called football. They call it this because you mostly use your feet to play. But you can touch the ball with any part of your body except your hands and arms.

7

Mom drives you to the soccer field, where your team, the Strikers, is warming up. Today the Strikers are playing the Comets.

Your coach has you and your teammates stretch your muscles. "Stretching is very important," she says. "You will be running a lot and want your muscles to be nice and loose."

A soccer field is a big grass rectangle with a goal on each end.

9

Your coach has you practice passing the ball to one another. "Call out the name of the person you are passing to," she says. "That way, your teammate will know the ball is coming."

When you kick the ball, use the inside of your foot or the top of your shoe. This will help you control the direction in which the ball travels.

Tyler calls Ashley's name and kicks the ball to her.

She stops the pass with the bottom of her shoe.

This is called a trap.

**Game time!** Coach places your team in its positions: four defenders, four midfielders, two forwards, and one goalkeeper. The four defenders help the goalkeeper stop the other team from scoring.

Midfielders help move the ball into the other team's half of the field. The forwards stay near the other team's goal and try to score. Coach picks you to be a forward.

Goalkeepers are the only players who can touch the ball with their hands and arms. Inside a special area around the goal, the goalkeeper can use his or her hands and arms to block shots, pick up the ball, and throw or roll the ball to teammates.

13

Each team lines up on its half of the field. The referee picks your team to start with the ball. She sets the ball in the middle of the field, blows her whistle, and starts the timer.

You dribble the ball by kicking it in front of you. Use both feet to dribble the ball, and keep the ball close to you.

Emily kicks the ball to Tyler, who dribbles it with his feet toward the other team's goal. "Spread out, Strikers!" your coach yells. "Get open for a pass!"

The Comets see Tyler dribbling toward them.
They try to stand between him and their goal.
One of the defenders blocks Tyler's path,
and he tries to dribble around her.

You can steal the ball from another player by getting close to that player and kicking the ball away. But be careful not to kick the other player. That is called a foul, which means it is against the rules.

She steals the ball and passes it to a Comets midfielder. He kicks the ball up in the air, high above the other players' heads.

The ball drops toward Sara, one of the Strikers' midfielders.

You can use an outside foot trap to stop a bouncing ball. As soon as the ball bounces, hit it with the outside of your foot. The ball should land beside you.

She traps the ball and passes it to you. You dribble toward the Comets' goalkeeper.

You dribble around two of the Comets' defenders.

Now only the goalkeeper is between you and the goal.

You bring your leg back. **WHACK!**

You kick the ball as hard as you

can toward the goal.

The goalkeeper dives toward your shot but can't reach the ball. It flies past him into the goal. **You scored!** The Strikers are ahead, 1-0. **Cheering, your teammates run to you.**

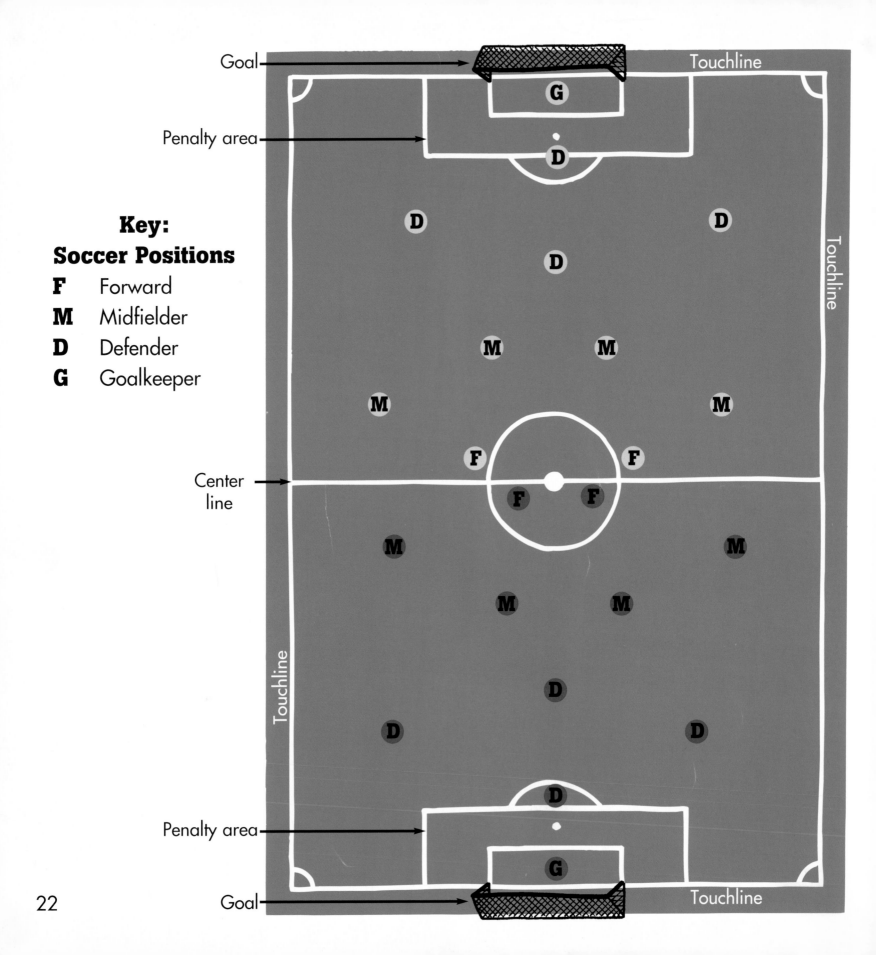

Goal

Touchline

**G**

Penalty area

**D**

**D** **D**

**D**

**Key:**
**Soccer Positions**

**F**    Forward

**M**   Midfielder

**D**   Defender

**G**   Goalkeeper

**M** **M**

Touchline

**M** **M**

**F** **F**

Center
line

**F** **F**

**M** **M**

**M** **M**

Touchline

**D**

**D** **D**

Penalty area

**D**

**G**

22

Goal

Touchline

# Fun Facts

 Games much like soccer have been played in many countries for hundreds of years. The Chinese played a game similar to soccer thousands of years ago! In the 1800s, the English invented rules for soccer as we know it today.

 Unlike games such as basketball and football, soccer games often do not see much scoring. Soccer also is one of the few sports that can end in a tie. Sometimes, nobody scores in an entire game!

 The biggest soccer tournament in the world is called the World Cup. It is played every four years.

 Mia Hamm, of the United States, is one of the most famous soccer players in the world. She is the leading goal scorer—for women *and* men—in international competition.

 Pele is a former professional soccer player from Brazil. During his career, Pele scored more than 1,200 goals. He is the only soccer player who has scored more than 1,000 goals as a professional.

# Glossary

**cleats**—special shoes worn to play soccer. Cleats have bumps on the bottom that help keep players from slipping on the grass.

**dribble**—to move the ball along by kicking it with your feet

**pass**—to kick the ball to a teammate

**steal**—to take the ball away from the other team

**trap**—to stop a pass with the bottom of your shoe

## To Learn More

### At the Library

Clark, Brooks. *Kids' Book of Soccer: Skills, Strategies, and the Rules of the Game.* Secaucus, N.J.: Carol Pub. Group, 1997.

Foreman, Michael. *Wonder Goal!* New York: Farrar, Straus Giroux, 2003.

Gibbons, Gail. *My Soccer Book.* New York: HarperCollins Publishers, 2000.

Goin, Kenn. *Soccer for Fun!* Minneapolis: Compass Point Books, 2003.

### On the Web

Fact Hound
Fact Hound offers a safe, fun way to find Web sites related to this book. All of the sites on Fact Hound have been researched by our staff. *http://www.facthound.com*

1. Visit the Fact Hound home page.

2. Enter a search word related to this book, or type in this special code:1404802622.

3. Click on the FETCH IT button.

Your trusty Fact Hound will fetch the best sites for you!

## Index

24